The Four Sublime States

The Brahmavihāras:
Contemplations on Love, Compassion,
Sympathetic Joy and Equanimity

David Tuffley

To my beloved Nation of Four
Concordia Domi – Foris Pax

But if you do not find an intelligent companion, a wise and well-behaved person going the same way as yourself, then go on your way alone, like a king abandoning a conquered kingdom, or like a great elephant in the deep forest – The Buddha.

Published 2012 by Altiora Publications
AltioraPublications.com/
ISBN-13: 978-1470053895   ISBN-10: 1470053896

Copyright © David Tuffley, 2012.

All rights reserved. Without limiting the rights under copyright reserved above, no part of this publication may be reproduced, stored in, or introduced into a retrieval system, or transmitted, in any form without the prior written permission of the copyright owner.

About the Author

David Tuffley PhD is a lecturer at Griffith University in Australia where he teaches philosophy.

Acknowledgements

Special thanks are due to my partner Angela for her unwavering support and encouragement.

Contents

INTRODUCTION 1
THE IMMEASURABLES 4
MEDITATIONS ON THE FOUR STATES 7
THE FOUR SUBLIME STATES 9
    LOVE 9
    COMPASSION 12
    SYMPATHETIC JOY 14
    EQUANIMITY 16
DYNAMIC INTERACTION OF THE SUBLIME STATES 24
ESSENTIAL TRUTH 28
    THE ESSENCE OF BUDDHISM 28
    THE FOUR NOBLE TRUTHS 29
        If you are alive, you will suffer *29*
        The cause of suffering is attachment *30*
        You can end suffering *31*
        End suffering by following the eight-fold path *32*
            Right View 33
            Right Intention 33
            Right Speech 34
            Right Action 35
            Right Livelihood 35
            Right Effort 36
            Right Mindfulness 37
            Right Concentration 38
EQUANIMITY AND THE TAO 39

Introduction

Many people have heard of the *Four Noble Truths* and the *Noble Eight-Fold Path*. These were the subject of the Buddha's first address after becoming enlightened. They rightly form the foundation of Buddhist thought and can be seen for reference in a later chapter called *Essential Truth*.

Fewer people have heard of the *Four Sublime States*. They naturally follow the Four Noble Truths because they describe how to achieve a divine state of mind that leads to the best possible relations with the world and everyone in it, *plus* liberation from the cycle of re-birth when your time comes to leave this life. Could there be a more worthy goal in life than this? The Buddha urged people to adopt these sublime states as their habitual state of mind, making them your living space, your abode.

The Four Sublime States are *benevolence, compassion, sympathetic happiness,* and *mental calmness*. This book outlines a practical way for you to cultivate these states of mind which have great practical value in how you relate to the world. They engender harmony and good-will with others and with society as a whole. They act as levellers of social barriers, and makes us feel generous towards others as we widen our circle of care to include everyone in the world, not just our immediate family and friends.

Though many people regard Buddhism as a religion, strictly speaking it is not, since it does not mention God or gods. It is a practical way to living your life that would be better described in the modern world as a blend of Psychology and Philosophy, making it admirably suited to everyone, everywhere regardless of their existing beliefs.

The Four Sublime States activate our *Highest Self*. Humans have a multi-layered brain, the product of our evolutionary journey. From the savage instincts of our far-distant reptilian ancestors, still present in out brain as the Limbic System, to our mammalian brain that nurtures its children, all the way up to the recently evolved frontal lobes that let us make choices that transcend our animal instincts. When we use this part of our brain, we are not only *conscious*, we are conscious of *being* conscious. No other creature on Earth has a brain that is setup for meta-cognition.

Neuroscience knows that the human brain is the most complex biological structure ever to have existed. Yes, those three pounds of grey matter sitting between your ears is a true wonder of creation, the current peak of four billion years of evolution. This book shows you how to use this magnificent instrument to something like its fullest potential.

By adopting the Four Sublime States we learn to habitually dwell in the highly evolved parts of the brain. The impulses

The Four Sublime States

of hatred and malice that come from the primitive parts of our brain are starved of attention and energy and become incompatible with our way of thinking.

The Immeasurables

Love, compassion, sympathetic joy and *equanimity* are also known as the Immeasurables because they are boundless and all-inclusive. The four states should be applied equally to everyone, not only to all people, but to all sentient creatures without bias. Towards people, there is no discrimination on the basis of class, culture, religious, sexual-orientation, age or any other criteria that people use to categorise the social environment. Towards animals, likewise no discrimination, for example to regard one animal as noble and another a nuisance, or one animal good only for slaughter and another worthy of an honoured place in our homes.

Daily meditation on the four states is how you can make them second nature, or more properly expressed, your *first* nature. It will take some time, but will be worth the effort. As the old saying goes; *good habits are hard to form but easy to live with, while bad habits are easy to form but hard to live with.* In time, they will come to pervade all aspects of your life.

The meditative method has two parts; the right direction of thought, and repetitive practice. It is a common sense approach of proceeding from easy to hard. For example, when meditating on loving kindness, begin by wishing for your own well-being. That should be easy. Then wish for the

The Four Sublime States

well-being of your nearest and dearest loved one's, also easy. Then proceed to people you like and respect, then those you merely tolerate, then those you actively dislike or consider an enemy. Proceed through all these people, beginning with yourself, wishing each of them happiness and good health, even your enemies. Your attitude of loving kindness spreads outwards like the ripples from a stone cast into a pond.

The ripple of benevolent energy inevitably reaches a barrier at the place where your dislike for a person or group makes it difficult for you to feel any benevolence towards them. That is the place where the process goes from being easy to being hard, the place where your current limits are. With repeated practice, the waves of benevolent energy radiating in all directions overwhelm the barriers, washing them away. Repetition is the key to success. In time, you can teach yourself to extend the same loving kindness as you feel for yourself and your loved ones to everyone in the world, including your enemies or people you do not like. Practice, practice and more practice.

With practice, over time, the size and power of the radiating wave of benevolence is such that it reaches all over the world and is stopped by nothing. Your benevolence is boundless, immeasurable.

Exactly the same method is used in relation to cultivating the other sublime states; compassion, sympathetic joy and equanimity.

The Four Sublime States

When your mind is thoroughly grounded in the four sublime states, you will see the world as it truly is; impermanent, without substance and prone to suffering. You see all this with a mind that is calm and pure, unselfish and benevolent. This is the state of mind that is the foundation for greater spiritual insight.

The effects of this kind of meditation is slow and cumulative. The more you do it, the more pervasive will be the effect on you. As the Buddha observed, *what a person considers and reflects upon for a long time, to that his mind will bend and incline.*

The Four Sublime States

Meditations on the Four States

The passages below are adapted from the original talks given by the Buddha on the subject of how to acquire the Four Sublime States through meditation practice.

It will be noticed that the same process is repeated for each of the Four Sublime States of mind. When one iteration is complete, the cycle begins again. The whole process is meant to be repeated many times a day, then the following day and so on for weeks, months and years.

In this way you become a beacon that radiates loving-kindness, compassion, sympathetic joy and equanimity to every part of the world, nourishing all sentient creatures equally. This is a state of mind that emulates the divine.

1. Fill your heart with *loving-kindness* and send it in all directions, first North, then South, then East and West. Your loving-kindness circles the Earth and leaves no place untouched. Your heart is filled with loving-kindness for all sentient creatures, equally and without favour. It is abundant and boundless, given freely for the benefit of all.

2. Fill your heart with *compassion* and send it in all directions, first North, then South, then East and West.

The Four Sublime States

Your compassion circles the Earth and leaves no place untouched. Your heart is filled with compassion for all sentient creatures, equally and without favour. It is abundant and boundless, given freely for the benefit of all.

3. Fill your heart with *sympathetic joy* and send it in all directions, first North, then South, then East and West. Your sympathetic joy circles the Earth and leaves no place untouched. Your heart is filled with sympathetic joy for all sentient creatures, equally and without favour. It is abundant and boundless, given freely for the benefit of all.

4. Fill your heart with *equanimity* and send it in all directions, first North, then South, then East and West. Your equanimity circles the Earth and leaves no place untouched. Your heart is filled with equanimity for all sentient creatures, equally and without favour. It is abundant and boundless, given freely for the benefit of all.

The Four Sublime States

This chapter explores the nature of each of the sublime states.

Love

The Love spoken of here is the self-less or unconditional love that has also been called *Agape* by the ancient Greeks. This is the highest expression of love, higher than *Philos* (friendship love) and *Eros* (erotic love).

This kind of Love wants others to prosper and be happy without wanting to possess them or expecting anything in return. Unconditional love is much the same as the sunshine that nourishes all life. It shines regardless of whether people appreciate its warmth, curses its brightness or ignores it altogether. Sunshine is indeed an emanation of divine love on the physical plane.

To love unconditionally, one must transcend the ego, the 'I'. The ego is an aspect of our total self that came into existence hundreds of thousands of years ago to help our ancestors devise survival strategies in a dangerous world. Of

The Four Sublime States

course it was selfish; its purpose was to keep us alive when all around was danger.

Today, we live in a civilised, law-governed world where much of the danger that previously existed and threatened our survival has long since been legislated away. We do not need the ego to survive now, but the ego *wants* to survive, and will resist all efforts to diminish it. When you try to transcend it, the ego fights back, determined to preserve its existence. The key is to understand that the ego is a sub-set of our overall self. It must not be allowed to dominate and define us. We are so much more than our ego.

This is a battle that cannot be fought and won in a single day. Once you recognise that the ego is a major impediment to your spiritual growth, your determination to grow can exert a constant pressure on the ego to bring it to heel over months and years. It may never disappear altogether and you may not want it to, because if you are living in the world (as opposed to living a cloistered or hermit-like existence) then you still need your ego to help you negotiate your way in the world and get things done. The challenge is to have your ego under the control of your Highest Self, not to have the ego be in charge of your life where it is certain to make you unhappy.

The unconditional love you feel for your child or partner should be extended out into the world to include everyone, even those people you do not like, or who do not like you. Therein lies the challenge. It is easy to altruistically love your

The Four Sublime States

baby, not so easy to feel that same love for a stranger on the other side of the world, particularly when that stranger lives in a filthy, far distant slum where people definitely need their egos to survive.

Love should be unconditional, since conditional love creates its own opposite, something you dislike or even hate. Unconditional love extends to all corners of the Earth, from the highest mountain to the deepest ocean, the coldest tundra to the hottest desert. There is nowhere that your love does not reach and permeate and nourish. Every creature from the slimy eel-like hag-fish feeding on the corpse of a whale on the bottom of the deep ocean, to the noble eagle soaring on the air currents above a pristine snow covered mountain, and every creature in between. It is easy to love the eagle, but what about the hag-fish, sometimes described by marine biologists as the most disgusting creature in the sea?

Unconditional love extends easily to the good and the noble, but it is the low-minded and the bad that are in the greatest need of love. Even in the worst, most evil person resides a spark of divinity that has been all-but extinguished by a loveless world. Yet, the near dead ember of divinity can be fanned back into a flame when the miracle of love comes its way. It is the same spark that resides in us all. Can you honestly say that you would not be like them were you to walk a mile in their shoes? The wise person understands this, and does not judge. They are human, just like everyone else, not sub-human. This is what the Buddha exhorts us to remember.

It is *Agape* (unconditional love) we want, not *Eros* (erotic love) that burns hot and sudden, but dies away quickly leaving us colder and lonelier than we were before. Agape is like a reassuring hand on the shoulder of a frightened person. In their confusion, the person might snarl at the hand, but no offence is taken. We wish only to bring comfort and healing; we do not expect gratitude.

Unconditional love has transcended the ego, and from this liberated position, we can see that people's suffering and confusion have been created by their controlling egos. We wish only to ease that suffering by giving them strength without expecting anything in return.

Unconditional love is the product of a liberated heart; it is the highest, most sublimely beautiful energy of all, and it leads to the cessation of suffering and enlightenment. It is truly divine, and you are capable of not just experiencing it in your own life, but also to generate vast amounts of it and send it out into the world. Resolve to do this!

Compassion

It is a fact that suffering exists in the world, the result of attachment to impermanence and delusion. Most people suffer for much of the time. So caught up in our own suffering can we become that we stop noticing the suffering

The Four Sublime States

of others. We do not hear their cries of distress. We become deaf to their pleas, and blind to their plight.

The selfish ego tells us it is not our problem. We must harden our hearts and isolate ourselves in the cold comfort of our fortress of solitude where the illusion of safety can be maintained. Like Alcatraz Island in San Francisco Bay, from the outside it is a picturesque fortress, but from the inside it is a prison, a place of great suffering.

Only by transcending the ego can we release ourselves from our prison, and having done so then be able to help others end *their* suffering. Compassion keeps the continual suffering of others vividly present in our minds, even at times when we ourselves are free from suffering. Compassion opens the heart, takes the blind-fold from our eyes, and opens our ears to the reality of a profoundly suffering world. This makes our own problems seem small.

The Irish playwright George Bernard Shaw said it most eloquently:

This is the true joy of life, the being used up for a purpose recognized by yourself as a mighty one; being a force of nature instead of a feverish, selfish little clod of ailments and grievances, complaining that the world will not devote itself to making you happy.

Compassion is empathy; the ability to go beyond our narrowly defined egoic self and put ourselves in someone else's skin, or in the minds of groups and communities and nations. We feel their suffering because we have willingly entered their world and made their suffering our own. We understand their suffering because we know that in countless previous lives we have been where they are now, have done what they are now doing. Knowing this, we understand and do not judge them.

If we do not learn from our experiences, we are doomed to repeat them until we *do* learn. If we lack compassion now, one day soon we shall find ourselves crying out for it. Better to cultivate it now.

The foundation of compassion is when you come to perceive the real causes of suffering; attachment to impermanence, delusional beliefs about the world, and selfish habits. When we see selfish, deluded people, we know that suffering is never far away. When we transcend our own egos and perceive this truth, compassion naturally follows.

Compassion is a defence against suffering. By being compassionate, we transcend the state of mind that creates suffering. Noble, serene, understanding, willing to help, empowering; these are the characteristics of true compassion that leads to the cessation of suffering and enlightenment.

Sympathetic Joy

The unevolved mind experiences little true happiness in life. It is trapped in a prison created by the selfish ego which

The Four Sublime States

feels itself to be separate from everything else in the world. This is a delusion since in reality everything in the universe is connected to everything else. To perceive yourself as separate is a primary cause of suffering. Enlightenment occurs when you experience a sense of felt-connectedness with everything.

When you feel happiness yourself, you want to share with everyone, particularly those whose lives are grim and joyless. When you observe happiness in others, you sympathetically share in it with them, being happy that they are happy. Happiness is a noble emotion. It transcends the self and inspires noble thoughts and actions.

It is a self-reinforcing feedback loop, the happier you make others, the happier you become. This is the essence of sympathetic joy.

Let us then make it our mission to bring as much happiness to as many people as possible. Let us do this by showing them how to find that joy within themselves. Their happiness becomes the source of your happiness.

True happiness helps you along the path of spiritual growth and the extinction of suffering. It can be achieved through becoming the fullest expression of your human potential, a process known as Self-Actualisation. This is a natural state of happiness, and one that is within the reach of everyone. It comes from having transcended your base nature.

This is the kind of happiness that cannot be obtained off the shelf through the acquisition of things. The fleeting gratification in receiving goods or services is not true happiness. That is an illusion created by our global consumer society

Happiness is a great help on the path to enlightenment, it calms the mind and allows us to have insight into spiritual truth that would not be possible with an unhappy mind. Such happiness is attained when you know that you have helped people find happiness through the cessation of suffering, and ultimately enlightenment. This is the nature of sympathetic joy.

Equanimity

Equanimity is balance, poise, equilibrium. It is the result the sustained effort needed to reach a level of understanding and insight into your own true nature, plus the self-discipline to avoid activities and ways of thinking that create unrest.

Achieving such balance is like tight-rope walking. It requires much practice, and careful, moment-by-moment awareness, plus the making of many micro-adjustments as you go along. No-one says it is easy. It takes patience, vigilance and sustained effort.

When you look at the world around you, notice how everything is cyclic. What is currently strong will become

The Four Sublime States

weak, then strong again. What is high becomes low then high. What is bright becomes dark then light. Is this not the pattern of night and day and the pattern of all life?

When we succeed, we are happy. When we fail, we are sad. Our emotions follow the pattern of events in lock-step. For many people, life is like a roller-coaster ride with many ups and downs. The wise person though looks for ways to smooth out the rises and falls so that they go along steadily.

In Taoism, this is known as finding the Middle Path. Following the Middle Path means avoiding extremes and always seeking the middle path on our journey through life. The objective is to negotiate the middle ground between opposites or extremes so effectively that no act is followed by a reaction. The net effect is one of neutrality. Finding the middle path means not needing to suffer the consequences of an act. In terms of the doctrine of Karma, it means knowing how to avoid bad reactions, or bad karma.

Equanimity means living so that we do not swing like a pendulum from one drama to the next, creating disturbances in our lives that get in the way of calm inner reflection. It is finding the Middle Path. We are encouraged to sense the world around us directly and to contemplate our impressions deeply. It is wise to not rely too much on the structures and belief systems that have been created by others and put forward as orthodox truth. Such ideologies remove us from a direct experience of life and effectively cut us off from our source of insight.

The Four Sublime States

The tranquil mind comes to understand that everything in the universe is in a state of flux, and that the emotional and intellectual structures that we like to build for ourselves in order to feel secure and understand the world are likewise subject to change by external forces that are largely beyond our control. The challenge is to accept the inevitability of change and not waste our energy trying to prop up these impermanent structures, defending them against criticisms, and convincing others to believe in them so that they might become recognised as permanent truth.

Equanimity means finding the Middle Path and keeping to it so that you are able to arrange your life so that enough peace and tranquillity exists in your inner world for the experience of enlightenment to occur. It is like calming the turbulent waves above a coral reef so you can see clearly down into the depths where the coral is revealed in all its beauty. The surface of the water *must* be calm. A person whose life is chaotic, lurching from one disaster to the next in a constant state of crisis cannot become enlightened because their mind, like the stormy sea, is too turbulent for insight to be possible.

With insight, we are able to see the cause and effect linkages that underpin our lives. You come to see that what you thought and did in the past has created your world today. Likewise, what you do today will create your world tomorrow. You become the engineer of your own future. You visualise the future you want, then trace back and know what causal actions need to be performed now in order for

The Four Sublime States

the future effect to come about. This is how any successful person operates, consciously performing good causal events (karma) now so that good effects occur in the future.

You also realise how futile it is to blame others for your situation when it is always within your power to choose which path to take which action to perform. Giving up your right to choose and letting someone else decide for you is still an act of choice on your part. You still have to take responsibility for the outcomes. Equanimity gives you the insight to see all this.

Equanimity helps you to understand that suffering can be instructive because it is the result of something we did in the past and if we can look back and see what that was (not always easy to discern), we have learned a valuable lesson. If your present suffering helps you to avoid future suffering, it is arguably a good thing.

A major impediment to the development of equanimity is the ego or sense of self. The ego destroys equanimity by being always ready to be judge, to claim ownership, to take offence. It stands ready to engage in battle at any moment. Adrenaline flows, making us ready for fight or flight. The ego is after all part of our primitive survival instinct. It did a good job helping our species strategise ways to survive, but now it is getting in the way of higher development. It must be brought under control and contained so that it does not create problems for us on the spiritual path.

The Four Sublime States

How does one transcend the ego? Remember that life is suffering due to attachment to impermanence. It is the ego that is attached to the things of this world. The degree of importance assigned to something, that is how attached you are to it, is determined by how important it is seen to be to your continued survival. So you transcend the ego by consciously giving up thoughts of possession. That is any thought that features the words *me, myself* and *I*. Begin with the small, unimportant things and gradually work your way up to the most important things in your life.

Ultimately you should have no attachment to anything. Only then will you have true equanimity. Be willing to let it all go. To lose a dollar out of your pocket is nothing. To lose out on that promotion is difficult but not impossible to accept. To lose your partner or your children is a catastrophe that does not bear thinking about, yet nothing is more certain in life that every person now alive will one day be dead. Is this morbid? No, it is simply a fact. Why delude yourself that it is not so? We should make every effort to keep our loved ones safe, but at the same time fully accept the reality that tomorrow they might be gone.

When a tornado takes your house, and a News reporter is asking you how they feel as you stand there beside the bare slab, you should be able to say, *oh well, it was just a house; at least I am still alive*. This is not the answer the reporter is hoping for. He is hoping for a *woe is me* response because the mainstream News media wants to strengthen people's sense of self, not diminish it.

The Four Sublime States

For example, in the early morning of December 13th, 1989 my wife and I were sitting in a Kombi campervan at the side of the A13, a main road between Dover and London in England. We had been travelling and living in the van for the previous six weeks, had been in Berlin when the wall was coming down.

With no warning at all, an 18 wheeler with a full load of gravel and a fatigued driver hit us at speed from behind. The force of the impact was stupefying. We found ourselves hurtling towards the muddy ditch at the side of the road.

The Four Sublime States

Time slowed down, I had gone into hyperawareness, a survival instinct that helps people take life-saving action in a crisis. I knew what had happened, and expected the truck to any moment roll right over the top of us, grinding us up as it went. It seemed inevitable but I kept steering for the ditch nonetheless. Even today, decades later, I can still hear the sound of tearing metal and the roar of the big diesel engine; a moment of absolute terror.

In that moment, unexpectedly, my consciousness dissociated from my fearful ego. I suddenly felt peaceful, liberated. Dying seemed like the beginning a new adventure.

Ten minutes later, after it was all over, and we alive, standing, looking at the wreck, I remember feeling grateful that we were still alive, even though we had lost our car, our house, most of our worldly possessions and for a short time even my ego. It was all OK, these were just things that could not go with me into the next life.

Whether you transcend your ego through gradual, disciplined practice, or through a sudden, catastrophic event, the resulting equanimity is the same.

Equanimity is the crowning virtue that sits atop the previous three; love, compassion and sympathetic joy. Having equanimity, being non-attached, makes you no less capable of loving kindness, compassion or sympathetic joy. It intensifies them because you are free to concentrate on them

The Four Sublime States

rather than needing to deal with endless dramas and battles in your inner and outer worlds.

Dynamic interaction of the Sublime States

It will be helpful for you, as one trying to cultivate the four states, to understand the nature of the dynamic interplay between them.

Unconditional love, being universal, prevents compassion from becoming specific in its application. Compassion should be applied to everyone, not just those we are partial towards.

Unconditional love imbues equanimity with the poise that helps you to always remain calm. Love is a boundless energy that informs everything you do, and that energy is tempered and made stronger by equanimity. Your insight is deepened. So is your ability to refrain from action when it is better to let events unfold. When you let events unfold without interference, you intuitively perceive the real meaning contained in that situation, uncoloured by the effects of your actions.

Compassion reminds love and sympathetic joy that while you might be happy here and now, that there are many people elsewhere who are still suffering, sometimes grievously so. These folk must not be forgotten. Joy and

The Four Sublime States

suffering co-exist right next to each other. Compassion will not allow you to become smug and complacent by reminding you that there is more suffering in the world than we are personally able to heal, and that this suffering will continue until all sentient creatures achieve Nirvana (absence of suffering). Compassion is the spur that causes love to widen its application. It also causes sympathetic joy to look for more places to experience itself. Thus compassion is a great facilitator of both love and joy. Compassion cautions equanimity from descending into indifference to the suffering of others. It tempers equanimity to constantly re-enter the battle to end suffering, thus strengthening equanimity greatly.

Just as compassion helps sympathetic joy from becoming smug, sympathetic joy helps compassion from being overwhelmed by so much suffering. Joy is a great healer for a distressed mind. Compassion is at constant risk of degenerating into a depressed state of mind. Joy is just the tonic it needs to remain buoyant in the face of such sorrow. Joy enlivens compassion, energises it.

Sympathetic joy bestows upon equanimity the mild-mannered, good-natured demeanour reminiscent of the Buddha. The subtle half-smile with which you greet the world despite knowing of the deep suffering that exists all around. Joy is the smile that comforts and gives hope to those who see it. It is mild because it is tempered by compassion that is aware of the existence of suffering. Your demeanour is a message of hope to all in need of comfort and healing.

The Four Sublime States

Equanimity, or calmness and serenity, is the self-control and the guiding influence for love, joy and compassion. From its calm and disciplined point of view, equanimity can see what direction to go, and knows what must be done. It tells the other three how to apply themselves, and how to avoid dissipating themselves to no good effect.

Equanimity bestows upon love the quality of loyalty and the virtue of patience (perhaps the greatest of the virtues). Fickleness is banished.

Equanimity gives compassion the courage it needs to swim in a sea of misery and not be drowned. It shows those who would help others how to go about this difficult task with love and patience.

Equanimity is therefore the sublime state that crowns the other three and lets them work in harmony with each other. It does this by being the stabilizer that helps the other three stay on the Middle Path. It is also the insight-giver that tells the others what is really going on and what they should do next. Love, compassion and sympathetic joy are vulnerable and do not last long by themselves. Alone, they tend to deteriorate and become debased. The strong and balanced nature of equanimity creates a protective space that allows the others to exist and to function harmoniously.

So it is that equanimity is the foundation for the other three sublime states, and that these feed back to equanimity the virtues that prevent it from becoming degraded itself.

The Four Sublime States

Love, compassion and sympathetic joy prevent equanimity from become boring and cold-hearted, indifferent to the suffering of others. When all four work together, the heart and mind of the person is full to the brim with dynamic healing energy that is the essence of the divine.

Such a mind is untroubled by random thoughts and petty considerations. The consciousness that flows through it is calm and majestic, like a mighty river fed from pure mountain springs. The river flows into the sea but the sea level does not rise because an equal amount of water has evaporated, become clouds, and then fallen as rain on the mountain again. This dynamic process illustrates the essence of equanimity.

With the four sublime states firmly established and working in dynamic harmony, mindfulness blends with faith, courage with serenity, and insight with strength of purpose. They combine to make you an unstoppable force of nature. You are no longer prone to being trapped in the labyrinth of your own base nature, you have risen above it.

Your mind becomes like a facetted jewel. The light that comes into it is reflected back out to the world as a beautiful focussed beam of light; healing, dynamic, divine.

The Four Sublime States

Essential Truth

Much has been written about Buddhism and how to practice it. Readers will have no difficulty finding hundreds of books on the topic. This chapter simply focuses on the essence of Buddhism, as expressed in the Four Noble Truths and the Eight-fold Path.

Buddhism is not a religion as such; it does not propose an external God. It does not seek to replace a person's existing religious beliefs, only to supplement them. The Buddha, in all likelihood, would rather his followers describe themselves simply as *Followers of The Way*.

The essence of Buddhism

The great Saint-Philosopher *Atisha di Pankara* was Bengali scholar of noble birth who settled in Tibet in the 11th Century CE. Atisha reintroduced Buddhism to Tibet after it had gone into serious decline under King Langdharma. He is credited with establishing Tibet as a centre of profound Buddhist learning. The list below is the distillation of his great insight into the essence of Buddhism:

The Four Sublime States

The greatest achievement is selflessness.
The greatest worth is self-mastery.
The greatest quality is seeking to serve others.
The greatest precept is continual awareness.
The greatest medicine is the emptiness of everything.
The greatest action is not conforming with the worlds ways.
The greatest magic is transmuting the passions.
The greatest generosity is non-attachment.
The greatest goodness is a peaceful mind.
The greatest patience is humility.
The greatest effort is not concerned with results.
The greatest meditation is a mind that lets go.
The greatest wisdom is seeing through appearances.

The Four Noble Truths

The Four Noble Truths are the essence of the Buddha's teaching. They are believed to be the basis of the first sermon that he gave after becoming enlightened.

If you are alive, you will suffer

We humans are imperfect creatures, and the world in which we live is also imperfect. As we journey through life we are certain to suffer physical pain from illness and injury, and emotional pain from a host of psychological factors. But not all of our time is spent suffering. Sometimes we experience pleasure and enjoyment. A pleasure-seeking person heightens their suffering because there is an expectation that there should not be suffering in the first place. This expectation leads to self-pity; *Its not fair! This shouldn't be happening! Why me?! Poor me!* The first noble truth therefore counsels people to regard suffering as unavoidable in the unenlightened state. When happiness comes along, enjoy it while it lasts because it will not be permanent. You should not hold onto it as if it were permanent.

The enlightened person fully accepts the reality and unavoidability of suffering so that when it occurs they do not increase the suffering through their resistance to it. Acceptance should not be interpreted as enjoyment in a masochistic sense. The enlightened person can take immediate action to end the suffering, but while it lasts, they simply allow it to be.

The cause of suffering is attachment

Being attached to any worldly thing always leads to suffering, since nothing in the world is permanent and any attachment to impermanence is certain to cause suffering. All worldly entities, like the egoic self, social structures, relationships, human lives and cultures are bound to pass away sooner or later. People in the unenlightened state naturally form attachments to these impermanent things, thus creating the foundation for suffering. The underlying cause of attachment is desire, which manifests in a multitude of ways; it can be desire for higher status, wealth, sexual gratification, popularity, food, comfort, more possessions of all kinds to name a few.

The enlightened person understands the mind's tendency to form attachments to worldly things, including, and perhaps most importantly, the concept of egoic self. They work daily to reduce this attachment, and recognise that while the objects of our desires were once life affirming goals that increased our chances of survival in a savage world back in humanity's evolutionary past, these days, in a civilised world of plenty these aspects of our more primitive self need to be eliminated if we are to progress.

You can end suffering

The third noble truth holds that you can end your suffering by eliminating desire for sensual gratification and breaking the attachments you have to the egoic self and any of the other conceptual structures that are the furniture of your life.

The enlightened person works towards the full extinction of all clinging and craving as a way of eventually achieving *Nirvana* (absence of desire, or the extinguishment of the fires of greed, hatred and delusion). They know that the price they pay for this blissful state is the extinction of the egoic self. With no ego left, there are no boundaries to the mind. The enlightened person experiencing Nirvana expands their awareness to embrace the entire world, their selflessness generating infinite compassion for all living creatures. Transcending the egoic self in this way is a prerequisite for escaping the cycle of re-birth.

End suffering by following the eight-fold path

The eight-fold path is how the Buddha recommends you go about ending your suffering. It is useful for anyone seeking to live a more moral life in this world of suffering. The eight aspects are interconnected so that they form an integrated whole. As such they do not need to be performed in any sequence.

The eight-fold path aims to improve your:

- **Wisdom** by practicing right view and intention
- **Ethical conduct** by practicing right speech, action and livelihood
- **Mental capabilities** by practicing right effort, mindfulness and concentration

These are powerful agents of transformation in a person's life if they are practiced diligently over time. The eight-fold

The Four Sublime States

path enables the seeker after Satori to cultivate the mind-set in which Satori can spontaneously occur.

Right View

The cultivation of Right View is about applying the four noble truths in your life, taking them from an abstract idea into a living reality. The enlightened person sees the truth of the world, recognising the flawed and temporary nature of objects and ideas. They see the cause and effect relationships that connect the events of the world (karma).

Because all ideas and concepts are ultimately impermanent, the enlightened person does not rely on ideologies and other external explanations of the world in order to practice Right View. Instead they cultivate their Intuition and use it to build a deeper, more complete understanding of the world beyond the level of appearances.

Right Intention

Humans are volitional creatures, able to exercise choice. Yet having the capability to make choices does not mean a person will exercise it. They might take the effortless route of allowing their base desires to guide their actions which requires little conscious thought. Right Intention is the commitment to become a more conscious person with a self-improvement mind-set. Upon this foundation of conscious self-improvement, the enlightened person creates an inner environment in which they consciously choose, moment-by-moment, the course of action that will help them become a better person.

The are three aspects to Right Intention; (a) *renunciation* where you resolve to resist the pull of various desires, (b) *good will* where you resolve to avoid indulging in anger, and (c) *harmlessness* where you resolve to do no harm and be compassionate.

Right Speech

Words can be powerful. Words can make or break a person's life, start wars or bring peace. Words can indeed be mightier than the sword, as great orators have proven. Right speech (including written words) is therefore the principle of always expressing oneself in a way that enhances the quality of people's lives, and does no harm. It means to refrain from (a) lies and deceit, (b) malicious language (including slander), (c) angry or offensive language, and (d) idle chit-chat (including gossip).

The enlightened person therefore tells the truth, speaks with warm gentleness when they do speak, and refrains from speaking when they have nothing important to say.

The Four Sublime States

Right Action

Right action can be defined in open-ended terms as that which a person should *not* do. That potentially leaves all else open. In broad terms, right action means refraining from (a) harming any sentient creature, (b) stealing, and (c) sexual misconduct. Doing no harm to others covers a very broad range of behaviours. The worst a person can do is to take the life of sentient creatures, hence many Buddhists are vegetarians. Not stealing includes all forms of robbery, theft, deceit and fraud; essentially taking what you have not earned the right to have.

The enlightened person is therefore a kind, compassionate person in their dealings with the world. They respect other people's property, and do not engage in sexual behaviour that harms others either at a physical or emotional level.

Right Livelihood

Right livelihood is about earning one's living in ways that do no harm to others. Of all the possible ways a person might earn money, they should avoid those that exploit people's weaknesses.

Right livelihood means one should refrain from any employment that is contrary to the principles of right action and right speech, including but not limited to (a) trading in weapons, (b) trading in living beings, including slavery, prostitution and raising animals for slaughter, (c) butchery and meat processing, and (d) trading in drugs and poisons, including alcohol and recreational drugs.

Right Effort

Right effort is being prepared to put in as much effort as is needed to live the noble truths and eight-fold path. Some people are inclined to ration how much effort they will exert, which effectively excludes them from many worthy endeavours that do not appear to have a big enough return on their effort. Right effort is an attitude of *I don't care how much effort it takes, I'm going to do it!* As such it underpins Right Intention.

The mental energy that is consumed by right effort is directed into self-discipline, truthfulness and compassion. The same energy might otherwise be channelled through a person's base nature to produce desire, aggression and violence. Right effort ensures that this mental energy is expressed in wholesome ways.

The enlightened person therefore practices right effort by (a) preventing unwholesome states of mind from arising in them, (b) releasing unwholesome states that have already arisen, (c) arousing wholesome states that have not already arisen, and (d) preserving wholesome states that have already arisen.

The Four Sublime States

Right Mindfulness

Right mindfulness is a state of heightened consciousness in which a person has cultivated the mental ability to see the world around them clearly, without delusion. Seeing the world clearly requires a person to allow sense perceptions to be received but not be thought about too much. Many people take a sense perception and immediately begin conceptualising and categorising it until a conclusion is reached after complex processing that bears little resemblance to external reality, having been filtered through the person's preconceived ideas. This process occurs more or less unconsciously in most people. Right mindfulness is therefore about becoming conscious of your mind's tendency to interpret and distort meaning from our experience of the world and work to limit this tendency.

The enlightened person has learned to observe their mind and control how it goes. They have cultivated *consciousness about consciousness*. It is doubtful whether any other creature on the planet is capable of meta-awareness, since it appears to be a function of the recently evolved portions of the human brain that other animals do not have. Exercising these higher brain functions does not happen automatically in most people, it must be cultivated through right mindfulness.

The enlightened person therefore cultivates right mindfulness through contemplating the four foundations; (a) the body, (b) one's feelings (repulsion, neutrality, attraction), (c) one's state of mind, and (d) observed phenomena.

Right Concentration

Right concentration is about developing the capability to focus all of one's attention on a single object and maintain that focus over an extended period. All of the aspects of the mind are unified and working towards this one activity. Conflicting and distracting mental processes have been eliminated or sublimated into the unified effort. The object of this concentration is on some aspect of the noble truths and eight-fold path. These are considered wholesome objects for right concentration.

The enlightened person cultivates right concentration through regular meditation practice.

The Four Sublime States

Equanimity and the Tao

Equanimity is the fourth sublime state of mind and the great enabler of the other three (love, compassion and sympathetic joy). To cultivate equanimity you must bring your life into a harmonious relationship with the world, with Nature. Taoist philosophy offers a helpful way of doing this.

A central idea in Taoism is avoiding extremes and always seeking the Middle Path on our journey through life. The objective is to negotiate the middle ground between opposites or extremes so effectively that no act is followed by a reaction. The net effect is one of neutrality. Finding the middle path means not needing to suffer the consequences of an act. In terms of the doctrine of Karma, it means knowing how to avoid bad reactions, or bad karma.

Equanimity means learning to live in this way so that we do not swing like a pendulum from one drama to the next, creating disturbances in our lives that get in the way of calm inner reflection. It is finding the Middle Path. You are encouraged to sense the world around you directly and to contemplate your impressions deeply. It advises against relying on the structures and belief systems that have been created by others and put forward as orthodox truth. Such ideologies remove you from a direct experience of life and effectively cut us off from our Intuition.

The Middle Path requires you to develop an awareness of the physical forces that shape your world and direct its events. Such forces operate uniformly at all levels, from the macrocosm to the microcosm. They operate in the universe as a whole and in the minds and lives of individual people. An understanding of these natural laws and the forces they direct gives you the power to direct events in the world without resorting to force, by using attitude instead of action. Influence on others is achieved through guiding rather than ruling. The objective is always to avoid taking action that will elicit counter-reactions. In Nature, an excessive force in a particular direction tends to trigger the growth of an opposing force, and therefore the use of force cannot be the basis for establishing an enduring social condition.

As you cultivate equanimity, you come to understand that everything in the universe is in a state of flux, and that the emotional and intellectual structures that we like to build for ourselves in order to feel secure and understand the world are likewise subject to change by external forces that are largely beyond our control. The challenge is to accept the inevitability of change and not waste our energy trying to prop up these impermanent structures, defending them against criticisms, and trying to convince others to believe in them so that they might become recognised as permanent truth.

The Four Sublime States

Grasping the reality of the impermanence of all structures allows us to align ourselves with the forces of Nature that bring about incremental change in the social and physical world. We can embrace and support change whenever and wherever it wants to occur. Our alignment with the forces in Nature makes us a part of those forces. Our perceptual processes become more finely tuned because they are based on evolving reality, not on orthodox thinking. We see the world as it is, not as we believe it should be.

Printed in Great Britain
by Amazon.co.uk, Ltd.,
Marston Gate.